Jarrold Butterflies Series Book 1
With text by **George E. Hyde**

British Butterflies
Book 1

D1825121

9780853064169

Jarrold Colour Publications, Norwich

In the early part of this century Richard South produced his celebrated volume in the Wayside and Woodland series covering British Butterflies in all their aspects. It was followed between the wars by F. W. Frohawk's classic treatise which concentrated on the life histories of these insects. In the forty years since this last work was published a great deal more has been learnt about the natural history and distribution of our Lepidoptera. A further and up-to-date comprehensive study of the butterflies in particular has been much needed for some time. No one could be better fitted than Mr George Hyde to undertake such work, and to bring together recently accumulated knowledge on this fascinating subject. There must be many naturalists and others who are already familiar with his previous books with their excellent studies by colour photography of almost all our butterfly species. The present work, contained in two modest books, is once more rich in fine illustrations, including some that deal with the early stages and development of the respective species. It will surely commend itself to all who have the preservation of our lepidopterous fauna at heart, and especially now that many of our butterflies are threatened by the ever increasing spread of industry, reafforestation and agriculture.

Charles G. M. de Worms

Of all the vast assortment of insects it is no exaggeration to say that butterflies are the most admired and popular because of their grace and beauty, also on account of their association with other attractions of gardens and countryside. Only a very limited number are in any way harmful, and they help to pollinate flowers. The world population of butterflies totals many thousands of species, and in Europe alone are found some 380 species, but Britain's modest total of no more than 70 species has probably given rise to more study and speculation than all the rest. A more serious interest in British butterflies commenced in the second half of the seventeenth century, and increased considerably in the eighteenth and nineteenth centuries. One of the earliest works on the subject is *Historia Insectorum* by John Ray, published in 1710, in which some 48 species of butterflies are mentioned. A later work, with fine hand-coloured plates, is *The Papilios of Great Britain* by W. Lewin, published in 1795. The plates were painted under the immediate direction of the author, and the text is in both English and French. Of more modern times is the very comprehensive and finely illustrated work in two large volumes, *The Natural History of British Butterflies* by F. W. Frohawk, published in 1924.

Apart from studying the habits and life cycle of butterflies, the perfect insects have been collected and preserved on a large scale, and although this is sometimes strongly criticised it is only fair to say that much of our present knowledge of butterflies is due to the efforts and records of collectors. This by no means excuses the wanton taking of large numbers of less common species, but in considering the recent reduction in our butterfly population it should be realised that some other destructive influences are more to blame. These include the reclamation and cultivation of so-called wasteland, the replacement of deciduous woodland by pine trees, and the never ending spread of urbanisation. In addition to this it should be remembered that butterflies are diurnal, and because of it more affected by weather than many other types of insects. A sunless summer or a cold spring can cause serious reductions in the number of individuals of even common species for the simple reason that most female butterflies deposit eggs only in bright weather. A prolonged dull spell leads to many eggs never being laid, with a resultant reduction in the number of caterpillars. A cold spring can also be very harmful to eggs laid in the previous year, and due to hatch in April or May, also to caterpillars that have hibernated in the winter. It will be obvious that every kind of butterfly living in this country must survive the winter in one stage or another. Only five species hibernate in the butterfly stage. The rest go through the winter in one or another of the other three stages. Both butterflies and moths, in common with many other types of insects, pass through what is termed a complete metamorphosis. This includes the four stages of ovum or egg, larva or caterpillar, pupa or chrysalis, imago or perfect insect. The duration of each stage varies very considerably in different species.

If we handle a butterfly carelessly our fingers will show traces of what appears to be coloured dust, but if this is magnified it will be found to consist of minute scales. The wings of both butterflies and moths are covered with very large numbers of scales which fit closely together like the slates or tiles on a roof. It is because of this that the name Lepidoptera, from the Greek *lepis*, a scale, and *pteron*, a wing, has been given to the insects. In observing different butterflies it will be obvious that some species resemble one another more than others. There is no need to go farther than a garden on a bright day in August to realise this, for if the conditions are favourable there might well be both kinds of common whites and also some coloured butterflies in close proximity on such flowers as buddleia and Michaelmas daisies, which are great favourites of the insects. The coloured species could include the handsome peacock, easily identified by its markings similar to those on a peacock's tail, and the lively small tortoiseshell which has tortoiseshell markings. The two are related, and belong to the family Nymphalidae which includes many more species. An interesting detail is that all members of this family, however much they differ in size or markings, have only two pairs of fully developed legs suitable for walking. The front legs are small and useless. The same applies to the different brown butterflies, such as the meadow brown, of the family Satyridae. White butterflies belong to yet another family, the Pieridae, and they have full use of all three pairs of legs.

As mentioned, few butterflies are harmful, and as far as British species are concerned there are only two, the large white and the small white. In this respect it should be realised that the butterflies themselves cause no damage as they are incapable of biting. When they visit flowers they are only seeking liquid refreshment in the form of nectar. If a butterfly on a flower is observed closely, its long flexible proboscis, or sucking-tube, will be seen as the insect probes the flower. When not required this useful organ is neatly coiled up like a watch spring underneath its owner's head. But returning to the harmful nature of the two common white butterflies, it is, of course, the caterpillars that cause damage by eating plants of the cabbage and nasturtium families. All the other British butterflies develop from caterpillars that feed on a wide variety of wild plants or trees, and do not normally eat cultivated plants. Another brightly coloured butterfly that frequently visits gardens is that favourite, the red admiral. Many people admire it, but not all are aware that it comes to Britain from abroad. It is true that red admirals breed here in summer, but the majority die when the cold weather starts. If it were not for immigration this species would not be seen in Britain. A number of other species looked upon as British are really aliens. Some readers might be surprised to learn that such frail looking insects as butterflies actually fly from country to country, but the truth is that migration in insects is by no means confined to butterflies. A number of different moths also found in Britain are only visitors, and amongst other types of insects that invade our shores are dragonflies.

Many who grow flowers are delighted to see coloured butterflies visiting them, and we sometimes hear the question, 'What will attract more butterflies?' As indicated before, buddleia flowers especially are beloved by butterflies, and in fact this popular shrub is often called the 'Butterfly Bush'. In late summer Michaelmas daisies attract the peacocks and small tortoiseshells as well as red admirals, and the same applies to the pink-flowered sedum often called the 'Ice Plant'. Is it possible to persuade butterflies to breed in the garden? Another common question. Well, this is not so easy unless an area of uncultivated ground is available. The white butterflies, of course, breed all too often in vegetable patches, but few gardeners would wish to encourage these pests. Red admirals, peacocks and small tortoiseshells all originate from caterpillars that feed on nettles, and will accept no other diet, so if there is a spare patch one might allow nettles to take over. A grass-covered area, not a lawn, which is left uncut throughout the year, might attract some of the commoner grass-feeding species such as the meadow brown and wall brown, of which the caterpillars eat grass, and hibernate in winter.

This book, and its companion book on butterflies, contains pictures from photographs of living subjects. These are mainly in colour and the two books include all the British butterflies. The names, both English and scientific, are given, also the names of the respective families. Most of the illustrations are well above natural size, but the actual wing-span, or other relevant measurement, is shown at the end of the single line captions. Following modern practice all measurements are given in millimetres.

1

The Milkweed butterfly is so called because its caterpillar feeds on milkweed, an American plant not found wild in Britain. Also known as the Monarch, the butterfly is the largest found in this country, but is a rare visitor from America. The first example was recorded in 1876, and since then upwards of 200 have been reported. The range of the species in America extends from Peru to Canada, and in some areas it is protected by law. Exactly how the butterflies reach Britain is something of a mystery, and it has been suggested that they are sometimes carried across the Atlantic Ocean in ships.

The Wall Brown, as the name implies, often settles on walls. It is a common species in much of England and Wales, also in southern Scotland, and appears twice in the year. The first brood of butterflies comes out in May, and the second appears in August. It belongs to the family Satyridae, or 'browns', of which no less than eleven species are found in Britain. All but one are mainly brown. The pale green caterpillars of the wall butterfly feed on grass by night.

Most butterflies love bright sunlight, but the Speckled Wood prefers shady pathways in woods and lanes. Two broods appear, in May and August respectively, and the species is common locally in much of England, Wales and Ireland . The Continental form of the butterfly is more tawny in colour.

1. **MILKWEED or MONARCH** *(Danaus plexippus)* Male 105 mm.
2. **WALL BROWN** *(Lasiommata megera)* Male 44 mm.
3. **SPECKLED WOOD** *(Parage aegeria)* Female 50 mm.

4

5

4. MOUNTAIN RINGLET *(Erebia epiphron)* Male 35 mm.

5. MARBLED WHITE *(Melanargia galathea)* Female 58 mm.

6. SCOTCH ARGUS *(Erebia aethiops)* Female 50 mm.

The small dark-winged Mountain Ringlet is our only alpine butterfly, and its restricted British haunts are in a limited part of the Lake District and central Scotland. Although reported from Ireland in the last century, there are apparently no recent records. It flies in sunshine, and is rarely seen much below 1,500 feet, in late June and July. The males look almost black, but the females have tawny markings on the wing borders.

The Marbled White is very different in appearance from the other species of browns and could be confused with true white butterflies. It appears in July and is found mainly in southern and western England, but survives in a few parts of Yorkshire. In common with its relations the marbled white walks on only four legs. Its markings do not usually vary very much, but all black and all white examples have been recorded.

As the name suggests, the Scotch Argus is found mainly north of the Scottish Border, but there are a few colonies of the species in remote areas in north-west England. The once famous colony at Grassington, Yorkshire, unfortunately no longer exists. The butterflies appear in early August and are remarkably local. They remain in close proximity in small areas even though adjacent ground is very similar. They fly only in sunshine, and hide amongst the grass in dull weather.

7

The main haunts of the Grayling butterfly are sandy heaths, chalk downs and sand dunes. Its range covers much of Britain and Ireland, but it has disappeared in recent years from some old haunts, notably in Lincolnshire. It rarely visits flowers, but spends much time resting on the ground with its wings tightly closed. Because of this it is easily overlooked or mistaken for a faded leaf. Some earlier butterfly collectors called it the 'Rock Butterfly'. A small race of the species is found locally in North Wales, and the butterflies are about one-third less in size than normal examples.

Until the last few years the Meadow Brown was regarded as one of our commonest butterflies, but its numbers have dwindled in many places. This is probably largely due to the destruction of old grassland. Although classed as single brooded, it can be seen from June to September, and its range covers all Britain and Ireland. The females are larger and brighter than the rather drab males.

The ring-shaped markings on the underside of the wings of the Ringlet butterfly have led to the popular name. It flies in grassy places in woods and lanes during July, and is well distributed in much of England and Wales, but more locally in Scotland and Ireland. The wing markings vary considerably, and in examples called variety *lanceolata* they are very elongated.

7. **GRAYLING** *(Hipparchia semele)* Male 56 mm.

8. **MEADOW BROWN** *(Maniola jurtina)* Female 55 mm.

9. **RINGLET** *(Aphantopus hyperantus)* Female 52 mm.

8

9

The Gatekeeper or Hedge Brown is often seen flitting around near gates and hedgerows during July, and the females are larger and of a paler brown than males. It is found in much of England and Wales, but less so in the north. Although reported from south Scotland there is doubt about its occurrence there, and it is found only sparingly in Ireland. The brownish caterpillar is rather similar in appearance to the caterpillar of the Scotch argus, but as the two are not found in the same places there is little danger of confusion.

Early writers on butterflies used the alternative names of Marsh Ringlet and Manchester Argus for the Large Heath butterfly, but the species vanished long ago from its original haunts at Chat Moss near Manchester. Today the species is found as far south as Shropshire, in North Wales, and more widely in Scotland and Ireland. The butterflies vary considerably in different localities, from the heavily marked sub-species *philoxenus* of Shropshire and Westmorland to the unspotted Scottish sub-species *Scotica*. The caterpillar is marked with two shades of green and matches the moorland grasses on which it feeds.

The Small Heath looks rather like a modest edition of the large heath, but its wings lack the markings of that species on the underside. It is well distributed and common in many grassy areas of Britain and Ireland.

11

12

10. **GATEKEEPER** *(Pyronia tithonus)* Male 40 mm.

11. **LARGE HEATH** *(Coenonympha tullia)* A pair 41–43 mm.

12. **SMALL HEATH** *(Coenonympha pamphilus)* Male 33 mm.

13

The Small Pearl-bordered Fritillary is one of nine species of fritillaries classed as British, and it belongs to the family Nymphalidae, which includes many more species. It is widely spread and commoner than some other fritillaries, and found in much of Britain. It flies in June and sometimes a small second brood appears in September. The caterpillars of the fritillaries are spine-covered, and several, including the present species, feed on violet.

The Queen of Spain Fritillary is not a native of Britain, but a rare visitor from Europe where it is common in some places. Most of the examples recorded here have been found in late summer, but they have been fewer in recent years. The species does not normally breed in this country, but occasionally eggs have been obtained from captured females and butterflies bred in captivity. A few years ago the author reared several examples in this way, and the caterpillars were fed on wild pansy. The butterflies emerged in November.

The Pearl-bordered Fritillary can be confused with the small pearl-bordered fritillary, and the two species sometimes fly together, But the difference is more obvious in the underside markings. The present species has fewer pearl-like spots, and is also slightly larger than its near relation, with wings of a paler fulvous brown colour.

13. SMALL PEARL-BORDERED FRITILLARY *(Clossiana selene)* Female 44 mm.

14. QUEEN OF SPAIN FRITILLARY *(Issoria lathonia)* Male 46 mm.

15. PEARL-BORDERED FRITILLARY *(Clossiana euphrosyne)* Male 44 mm.

14

15

16

17

16. DARK GREEN FRITILLARY *(Mesoacidalia aglaja)* Female 69 mm.

17. SILVER-WASHED FRITILLARY *(Argynnis paphia)* Male 72 mm.

18. HIGH BROWN FRITILLARY *(Fabriciana adippe)* Male 60 mm.

The Dark Green Fritillary is our commonest large fritillary, and the one most often seen. Its main haunts are in open country, but it is also found in some woods. It flies in July, and its range includes most of Britain and parts of Ireland. In recent years it has become scarcer in many areas in which it was once common. The females are noticeably larger than the males, and also more varied in colour. Some have a blackish appearance, but extreme varieties are rare. The green is on the underside of the hind wings.

Our largest fritillary, the Silver-washed, owes its name to the silvery markings on the underside. It flies in July and is found mainly, though not exclusively, in woodland. The females are paler than the males, and lack the heavy black scales, *androconia*, on the fore wings. A dark greenish variety of the female called *valezina* is found chiefly in the New Forest. The butterfly's main haunts are in the south of England, but it is common in parts of Ireland.

The High Brown Fritillary is apt to be confused with the dark green fritillary, especially the males, but it is found more often in woods. Its haunts, too, are more restricted, and mainly in southern England, although it is found in a few parts of Westmorland and north Lancashire. The caterpillars of these three species feed on violet leaves.

19. HEATH FRITILLARY *(Mellicta athalia)* Male 40 mm.

20. MARSH FRITILLARY *(Euphydryas aurinia)* Female 48 mm.

21. GLANVILLE FRITILLARY *(Melitaea cinxia)* Male 41 mm.

19

20

The common name of the Heath Fritillary is misleading for the butterfly is found in woods where cow-wheat grows freely. It flies in June, and is one of our rarer species, being confined to limited areas of Kent, Essex, Sussex and Devon. In earlier times it was found in more counties, including Oxfordshire. The caterpillars feed on cow-wheat and are gregarious when young. They hibernate in winter inside a common web, and recommence feeding in spring. They are very lively in sunshine and it is believed that game-birds prey heavily on them.

The Marsh Fritillary is also known as the Greasy Fritillary because of its shiny appearance. It flies in June and is well distributed locally in Britain and Ireland where its foodplant, the devil's bit scabious, is common. The more brightly coloured race, *praeclara*, is found mainly in Ireland. Although some strong colonies exist, this species tends to fluctuate in numbers from year to year, and has recently disappeared entirely from areas where it was once common.

The Glanville Fritillary was found formerly on the Kentish coast, but is now confined to the Isle of Wight. It can be seen in areas of rough ground mainly on sections of the 'undercliff' on the south coast, and it flies in June. The black caterpillars have contrasting red heads, and are gregarious. They feed on narrow-leaved plantain.

The Painted Lady butterfly is noted for swift flight and migration. Although some-times common in Britain it is not a native, but comes here from North Africa. Its range abroad is very wide and includes parts of America. Female painted ladies lay their eggs on thistle plants, and a generation of butterflies develops later in the summer, but the species cannot survive our winter. The spiny caterpillars feed on thistles and occasionally on nettles. They construct silken shelters amongst the leaves in which to hide.

The handsome Red Admiral is a popular visitor to gardens, and is often seen on buddleias and Michaelmas daisies, but it is another alien. In common with the painted lady its true home is in North Africa, and it migrates from there to Britain and other countries. The caterpillars feed on nettle, and make silken shelters amongst the leaves. The butterfly occasionally survives our winter, but never in sufficient numbers to maintain a breeding stock here.

A glance at the tortoiseshell markings on the wings of the Small Tortoiseshell will reveal why the butterfly was given this name. It is our commonest brightly coloured butterfly, and often gets called the 'French Butterfly'. Its range covers nearly all Britain and Ireland, and it can be seen on the wing from April until November. It hibernates in winter. The spiny caterpillars live in colonies.

23

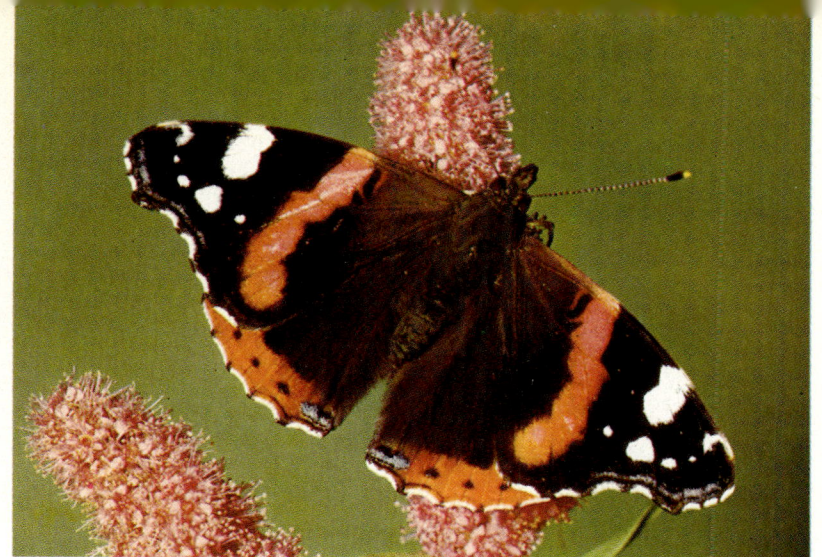

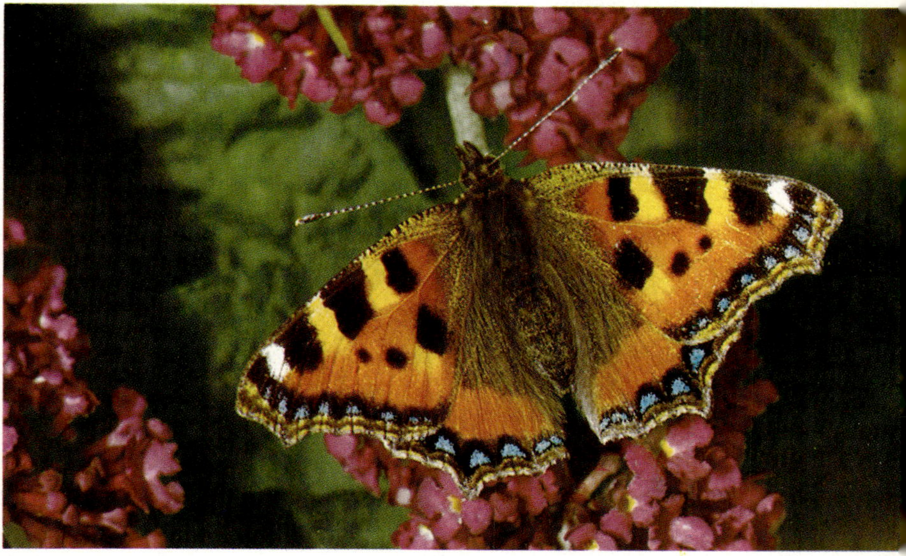

24

22. PAINTED LADY *(Vanessa cardui)* Male 64 mm.

23. RED ADMIRAL *(Vanessa atalanta)* Male 67 mm.

24. SMALL TORTOISESHELL *(Aglais urticae)* Male 50 mm.

25

Until about thirty years ago the Large Tortoiseshell was reasonably well established in parts of Essex and Suffolk, but it seems to have vanished from there and is now one of our rarest butterflies. In earlier times it had a much wider distribution in England and was found as far north as Yorkshire. Its chief haunts are tree-lined lanes and the verges of woods. The caterpillars are gregarious and feed mainly on elm, but they are greatly affected by ichneumon fly larvae which could account for the scarcity of the butterfly today. The butterflies hibernate in winter.

The Peacock is another common bright butterfly that visits gardens, and it is found in much of Britain and Ireland. It is easily identified by the conspicuous large blue spot on each wing, but in contrast its underside is almost black. The species is another of our five butterflies that hibernate in winter in such retreats as hollow trees and outbuildings. The black very spiny caterpillars feed in company on nettle.

The Camberwell Beauty was originally called the 'Mourning Cloak', and it has always been prized by butterfly collectors. It is a rare visitor to Britain, however, and does not breed here, which is strange as its caterpillars feed on willow, a common tree. The butterflies are found more commonly in parts of Europe, including Scandinavia.

25. LARGE TORTOISESHELL *(Nymphalis polychloros)* Female 70 mm.

26. PEACOCK *(Inachis io)* Male 63 mm.

27. CAMBERWELL BEAUTY *(Nymphalis antiopa)* Male 70 mm.

26

27

28

29

28. **COMMA** *(Polygonia c-album)* Male 55 mm.

29. **COMMA** *(Polygonia c-album)* Female resting 60 mm.

30. **PURPLE EMPEROR** *(Apatura iris)* Male 76 mm.

The Comma butterfly is easily recognised by its jagged appearance on the wing edges and also the white likeness of the letter C on the underside of each hind wing. It is a lively insect and not easily caught, but it has a trick of returning to a favourite perch even after being disturbed. In the early years of this century it was found mainly in the counties of Gloucestershire and Herefordshire, but more recently its range has been extended eastward and northward. It is now found as far north as Yorkshire, but is uncommon there. The caterpillar feeds on nettle and also wild hop, and there are two broods of butterflies each summer. Some have paler wings than others, and are called variety *hutchinsoni*.

The Purple Emperor is our largest indigenous butterfly apart from the swallow-tail, and the female, which is larger than the male, has a wing-span of some 84 mm. The two are much alike in general markings, but only the male has the purple sheen which has led to the popular name. The species is generally regarded as rare, but this is partly due to its elusive habits. The males spend much of the time around the tops of trees, especially oaks, in their wooded haunts. These are mainly in southern England, but the species is found as far north as Northampton-shire. A rare variety of this butterfly called *iole* lacks the normal white spots and bands on the wings.

As already mentioned, male purple emperors resort to the tree tops where they are easily overlooked. They do not visit flowers for refreshment like other butterflies, but sometimes take a drink from muddy puddles in the woods. They also visit carrion in the form of small dead animals, such as rabbits and stoats, lying on the ground. Some early butterfly collectors made use of such corpses to lure male purple emperors within reach of the net, but the females cannot be attracted in that way. They are more likely to be seen amongst sallow bushes where, after pairing, they lay their eggs. These are deposited on the upper surface of the leaves, usually only one egg on a leaf, and they hatch in about a fortnight. The young caterpillar feeds slowly on sallow leaves until autumn, and then settles down for the winter. It hibernates on a twig of the sallow, close to a bud, and its colour changes from green to olive-brown to match that of the bud. On completing its growth in the spring the caterpillar measures up to 48 mm. long, and it then prepares for the change into a pupa. As the picture shows it is shaped like a slug, and has a pair of stiff horns extending from the front of the head, which makes it unique amongst British caterpillars. The butterfly emerges about three weeks later. When the species is reared in captivity the caterpillar sometimes goes on feeding and the butterfly develops in autumn.

31

32

33

31. **PURPLE EMPEROR** *(Apatura iris)* Female resting 84 mm.

32. **PURPLE EMPEROR** *(Apatura iris)* Caterpillar fully grown 42–48 mm. long.

33. **PURPLE EMPEROR** *(Apatura iris)* Female pupa 33 mm. long.

34. **DUKE OF BURGUNDY FRITILLARY** *(Hamearis lucina)* Female 32 mm.

35. **WHITE ADMIRAL** *(Limenitis camilla)* Caterpillar 27–30 mm. long.

36. **WHITE ADMIRAL** *(Limenitis camilla)* Female 64 mm.

34

35

Although the Duke of Burgundy is called a fritillary it is not a true fritillary, but the sole member in this country of the family Nemeobriidae. It comes out in May and is found mainly in open woods where cowslips, the foodplant of the louse-shaped caterpillars, are plentiful. Although commonest locally in some southern counties its range extends as far as the Lake District. An interesting detail about the butterflies is that although the males have only two pairs of useful legs the females walk on all three pairs. The pupal stage lasts in a normal way from July until the next spring.

Of all our woodland butterflies, the White Admiral is the most graceful in flight and is greatly admired. Its haunts are mainly older woods, but it is also found in some more recently planted pine woods where honeysuckle, the food-plant of the caterpillar, is found commonly. It flies in June and July and its present range includes much of southern England, also extending as far north as Lincoln where, however, its numbers have declined in the last few years. The sexes are much alike in appearance, but the female is a little larger than the male. The cater-pillar hibernates while still small from October until April, and completes its growth in May. The pupa is marked with green and purple, and also has an attrac-tive golden sheen. It hangs head downward from a leaf or stem.

37
38

37. **SMALL BLUE** *(Cupido minimus)* Male 24 mm.

38. **LONG-TAILED BLUE** *(Lampides boeticus)* Male 34 mm.

39. **MAZARINE BLUE** *(Cyaniris semiargus)* Males **a** and **c**, Female **b** 36 mm.
    SHORT-TAILED BLUE *(Everes argiades)* Males **d** and **e** 23 mm.

The family Lycaenidae includes eighteen species of blues, coppers and hair-streaks, of which the caterpillars are all shaped like woodlice. The Small Blue or Little Blue is our smallest butterfly, with a wing-span of only 24 mm. It forms colonies and is found locally in much of southern England and in a few northern areas in parts of east Yorkshire and Scotland and also Ireland. In many of these localities it appears in June only, but in others there is a small second brood.

The Long-tailed Blue is a rare visitor to Britain and very few examples have been recorded in the last century, but it is common in some European countries. It breeds occasionally, however, and the caterpillars feed on the unripe seeds of everlasting pea and allied plants.

Three mounted specimens are shown of the Mazarine Blue which apparently became extinct in Britain about ninety years ago, but it was regarded as a rarity even by the very early butterfly collectors. Its former haunts were mainly in Dorset, but included Lincolnshire. Sexual difference in this species, as in some other blues is very obvious as the females are brown in contrast to the blue males.

The Short-tailed Blue is the rarest of all the casual migratory butterflies to reach Britain. It can easily be overlooked because of its small size, or mistaken for the silver-studded blue.

a

b

c

d

e

40. BROWN ARGUS *(Aricia agestis)* Female 29 mm.

40

Both sexes of the Brown Argus are deep brown with orange spots, but they show no traces of blue. There are two broods of the butterflies, in May–June and August–September respectively. The species is fairly widespread in southern England, and in the Midlands and much of Wales, though less common than formerly in some places. The allied sub-species *artaxerxers* is found locally in Scotland only. It can easily be recognised by the white dot on each fore wing. Another sub-species, called *salmacis* by Stevens, is found in County Durham, parts of Yorkshire and in other northern counties.